Brilliant Omnisquanderbus

Matt Prudhoe

the voidery aperture

First published in the United Kingdom in 2016
by
the Voidery Aperture

www.thevoideryaperture.com

All rights reserved

Copyright © Matt Prudhoe, 2016

Matt Prudhoe has asserted his right to be identified as author of this work in accordance with the Copyright, Designs and Patents Act, 1988.

ISBN 978-0-9954812-1-3

Contents

On sand	1
A partial success for the aggregate	2
Plenty	3
Don't look	4
Bathsheba at her toilet	5
Outlet	6
A bunch of keys	8
The siege	10
Human/traffic	12
Landscape with idiot	13
Windfall	15
Ground	17
Welcome to the union of unions	23
After that sojourn	25
Verbatim	26
Expectorant	27
Awash	28
Proposal for a superstructure	29
At the parting of the dogs	30
Dialogic	32
Posterity, here, for all good people, now	33
Didactic	38
Z new observance	40
Where is it, that silence	42
Gesture	44

On sand

Marram grass and the stunted
where the listening out
is for. Everything rooted
in the dry spillage. Why are you
shouting or did I mistake
it and you were a grunt
as he swung or whatever they do
on the golf course at the end
of it all just there. What's that
pocketed in the near unseen,
what masticator
poised above extinction.
How much longer for the acres
of conservatories, that pounding,
chainsaws braying from driveway
to driveway, and that decking
which was coveted and is redundant
and ought to be killed.

Fattened exhaust notes finger the distance.

Something close is crawling loudly into the sea.

A partial success for the aggregate

In desperate colloquy so to speak,
but our legs were doing what good legs do,
our legs were carrying all before them,
even the slowly distorting lenses of vitreous heat,
the hardening mucus enforcing the outlines,
even the quickening scrollwork of *muscae volitantes*,
things to be borne. But there were sinkholes
opening up beneath the pavements
and behind the armoured shop-fronts,
while an assembly of improvised blades was probing
with diligence all along the vulnerable edges.
For the record let's say that a gust or was it a blast
of dust or grit or something came funnelling down
and somewhere else there were deaths
and it was hard to discern with clarity what was meant
by any new workflow to which we might have referred
our attention. We were collectively perplexed but all
appropriate channels were open, very much open,
we'd been told. I noticed she'd painted her eyelids shut,
but still the mouth obligingly went on doing its business –
more effectively, if we're going to try to be honest,
than the reflexives which it managed to solicit,
in return, for the ears and brain. There were no sinkholes
except in the wilderness and the headlines. If it were subject
to independent verification it might be seen that
nothing had happened. That nothing would happen.
I had known her and you were she
and we were proceeding, the workflow
proceeding, as before, in desperate colloquy
so to speak.

Plenty

Last, the steel-rimmed gourd,
but not the right shape, and by definition
not from a goat. Plied with nitrates. Graced
with half-cut prayers and cribbed in the stolen incubator,
raid-proof, stowed in the loft. Retrieved, licked clean,
passed round and pressed to every cheek, the smeary
fingerprints and smudges nothing seedy to a normal healthy
normal human being with normal healthy human appetites –
not in this light. Shaken and poured. Spilled
on the floor. Bunged with a dead friend's cod-grey laundry wad,
importuned, buried, violated, trawled
through unnameable substances
in hot-tub, fish-tank, bog.
Buffed to a sheen. Left
in the sun. Pronounced replenished.
Fought over nightly
for downing in one.

Don't look

A mouth was shouting at itself – stuff about love,
small hatreds, sexual maturity – in the wilderness of
someone else's leisure, often howling, sometimes laughing,
now and then screaming, but no-one was listening. No-one
was listening but many could hear it and some
were paying to smear themselves liberally
in the spatter, the passionate spit.

You could have stared at a wall, content
to stare at a wall, but they were fingering the mortar
on the outside, probing the weak points, hollowing conduits
for their risible coloratura, pleading, tears, as though you cared
about that lifelong burning craving, solemn legacy
of that carjacked dog, regurgitated gran,
those bartered kidneys, feasting flies.

Still, what's a wall but rubble in waiting, what
but brick dust in denial? You might have shared that asininity,
given it lips, a couple of teeth and a tongue in the void,
except that no-one would have been listening, no-one anywhere
would have troubled you with a reply. Quite a result, that.
Quite a result, now everyone matters. Everyone matters
here. Even more than everyone else, no-one replied.

Bathsheba at her toilet

Maggots in the raisin bread, presumption
of worms in the dog, the crimson sashes
chasing soot from hearthside flags, a vulpine softness,
mildew overlaying mildew deep in the folds, so much
distraction from the pending gift, the offering, all three
swollen teats descending, fat glazed badges of the nipples
iridescent with infection, seeking still the upturned face,
the clumsy gallantry, some unthinking affirmation
of life without end, as though the passage of time
might season as well as destroy, and none of it proof
against the riddle at the crux of a mutual vanity,
none of it proof against the future or the answer
to the riddle, *surgical waste*, and still, even now,
the urge to assay that ancient sacrament, wire-jawed,
straining to taste the shower-drops beading the skin,
the water inexplicably stale, the face reflected in them
inexplicably grey, the disabusing of *naïveté*
already a fading image: broken pottery, dust, a heap
of suspect bedclothes, tragic sandals next to the bathtub,
three jars of unction, a bottle of pills.

Outlet

No-one here says sorry, needs
to account for. Crud heeled in – the car
outside, we mean, inside it – just another way
of showing that you owe us. Meat wagon,
milk float. Raised on breeze blocks.
Watch their bones, their skin – hard
edges. Someone's job
not been done properly. Us,
we're blameless.

Seek approval for the children,
from the children. We were once,
before this feast, this state, this thing they call a wondrous
what they call it, as we look on, fading,
half-lives of our ancestors – the near ones. Try to fit
our fuzzy outlines to their stains
burned onto pavements we remember
from our childhoods. How we skipped, or
kicked a ball. They
skip, kick a ball.

A free balloon with every
rush of sugar and gloop and wide-eyed
shock incomprehension accusations
things get broken quite unjustified
complaints about noise and filth. We say
you try it. Sacrificed more than you can know,
whatever we thought we were
we aren't it seems, you wouldn't understand,
you being unsplit and undecoded but hardly
unspoilt. Ethically sourced, they claim, the protein
marinating in our acids. And that explosion
they predicted – not just yet. They must have been lying.

Fuel conveying still more fuel, and life more life,
and life more death, the stinking disposables
they deal with somewhere else. Not to be spoken of
with your mouth full, not through a mouthful
of tumour and chips. Just doing our best. All
that we did back there
was our best.

A bunch of keys

It must have been quite a thing to see:
all spindle and clunk, spectacular waywardness
of grooved and chiselled metals, a mismatch of spokes
too much of a clumsy jostle to lace or true any rim,
a clutter of rotor blades too jagged to fly but just about
able to sail. The stark machinery of mishap, slowly
revolving, imparting some vague apprehension
of tragedy (mundane tragedy) as it traced its improvised arc
through foetid night air. This took place in the sinister
underpass, we should note. And its black leather wings,
spread out, not even a useless parody of flapping,
but not unappealingly so. Yes, quite a thing
to see. But as for the downturn, which began
a matter of mere but terrible inches just beyond
the arm that strained for it in vain, and then the fall,
the stunning hard plash on the concrete floor,
the brass and silver shingled in puddles of actual
piss, and how she scrabbled about on her knees
or how he scrabbled about on his knees
to scrape together again the means of all
that gave access to what had been earned
and was essential in that life, and what with no-one
to watch her back, or watch his back,
and given the knowledge of recent attacks – well,
you can imagine. But if you'd witnessed, too,
the naked unguarded expression of whatever it was
expressing itself unguarded and naked in every
stretch and grasp, and if you'd mused
on the implications of that, and found
your musings wanting, found them good,
or found them anything other
than nothing to do with anything
other than some poor sod's misfortune

in an underpass puddled with piss,
you might have seen fit, perhaps, to relent a bit,
neglecting to polish the key to the lock
that opened the door to the room
that no longer exists,
                        recording only
how the frantic glance was quenched
in the retrieval of the farthest key,
the leather folded tenderly, the press studs
softly pushed home.

The siege

All the contradictions have been noted.
We have made ironical statements, even
offered you vernacular *jeux d'esprit* in various idioms
from the folksy to the mildly pornographic,
and have resorted, not without irony,
but apparently without irony – this
was the irony – to a number of well-worn
bromides, some of which have been observed
to make the lips peel back from the teeth,
although their use is beyond all doubt
egalitarian. Perhaps the lips peeling back
from the teeth was a smile of approval
but the fact is no-one complained and there was nothing
to complain about, the hacks were doing their best
and we had kept a dialogue going, people
were talking and talking is good and why
should anyone take exception to the use
of so innocuous a phrase? *Siege mentality*,
that was one, and we for one would not
be ashamed to defend its employment. What else
to call habituation to the daily drill
of guilty palpitations, truing of aim
by squinting like experts down the soiled
shafts of their telescopes and truncheons
for the gruelling red-eyed vigilance of the long game
as it played between their episodic lapses
into boozy paraphilia? How else indeed. Only
the lottery, tossed for weekly. Prize a trip
around the buttresses at dawn with mallet and chisel,
charged to chip whatever mortar could be chipped
from under the stone the sap the week before had been trying
to undercut the moment they got him. Or got her.
It could have been her. Of the remains the students

excavated on site, a small proportion
was found to show female characteristics. When we say 'show'
we mean 'exhibit'. Make of that fact what you will.
Consider, too, the slight predominance of rubber
balaclavas over silk ones. Many died and no-one realized
that the buttresses, the walls, they didn't
realize that they hadn't — or which side of them they —
anyway, it was terrible. We've established
that. We've done our terrible duty to the past
and to the future. And you are our future. Your objections
have been noted. You may view them with irony [here]().

Human/traffic

Not the untenable soul,
this faint scintilla of something genuinely
vile concealed in the structure of the gesture
(almost a gesture), in the shellac stare,
redaction of the eyeball; not even the gaping
lacuna proposed to have taken its place,
that homicidal default they parachute
into the godless field for the hell of it
when they want to stoke the debate; not mere
nothingness; more like a deadness; worse,
the indefensible bullet-hard conviction
that such deadness must exist in perpetual
synthesis (hint of a paradox here) with animal spirits,
smooth accuracy in the firing of the circuits
that prompt the hand to flick the switchgear
in the instant the lights are seen to change to green,

as when they go wading into the shallows
and the murderous plunge into history comes
and nothing is too vile to be resisted,
or they stand by, watching the bodies go in,
the bodies coming back out again, going back in again,
not coming back.

And nothing seems up to it,
saying enough but not too much
about the process, the connection, if there's
process, if there's connection, if it's untenable,
indefensible, if you can speak of it, nothing and no-one
seems up to the task.

And what exactly was the task?

Landscape with idiot

This road,
    which is subsiding in the everyday manner
    of other such roads you'll never walk again.

And this sky,
    which may be everywhere at once
    but is in this winced-out moment only.

Also this rain,
    which hasn't come organized for rain
    and is leaving already.

When you forget to look
    it's not there,
    when you think about how to fix it in place
    you're not there either,

asking who else's shoes
    are more deserving of footsteps to be taken
    never again
    when this gravel attests a billion years or more
    of waiting,

who else on earth
    is so sporadic by virtue of trying
    to be present,
    who so present by virtue of promising
    not to come back,

if not merely everyone –
    all the perks of geolocation
    or its lack, the slip
    unrestricted to those who left behind the codes
    for cartoon faces
    floating off

Windfall

Derived from the palpable
sense of a ritual sparsely
attended: something like
inventory, circadian, global,
an audit in secret of every facile
diversion, every practical
joke in risible, flimsy solidity
played on the credulous,
just so, all of the gullible lightly
absolved of the obloquy,
honest participants, hefting
the weal still, good little turds.
Derived from that. Only tentative,
the something like, the sense
of a not even palpable in truth,
the warped and splintering
infinity of the edifice
staunched convincingly enough
with promissory notes
for dividends laudable enough
to keep it from sinking
in the dark and fertile sludge
of the not yet living – hypothetical
mewling descendants adduced
with reverence when it suits,
convenient recourse
in public dilemmas with moral dimensions,
innocent futures traded in
for jingles and stylish processions of light
with which to console ourselves
in the sentimental purgatory
of their absence, their becoming,
possible neverness, howling

shibboleths in whose honour
the inaugural barbecue, lit
long ago, we stoke with due care,
without caring.

Ground

Glints among the grass clumps,
polymeric in their bauble-cheery
almost-mineral not-quite-vulgar brightness,
as though we had something – we
being no-one, singular, heightened awareness
of grassness, awareness of grass – the clumps
by no means of the essence – something
to laugh about. Laugh about? Joke about.
Bracken was meant to be a carcinogen, once,
in sheep. They troubled to say. For now,
the blackening ushers what's left of these frail structures
into a hoisted microporosity, stowing the fragments;
this is a crumbling which is general and,
while part of the essence, by no means
part of the joke.

*

Only we lived somehow
then otherwise
won't know the half of it
even afterwards
don't know the half of it

what was the half of it
which and of what

*

But what of the rake-up, its rattle
and drift, the leaves fresh fallen,
wetness and squeak of an old incumbency
apparently restored in a formative delving,
nothing to see here,
merely a teeming of architectural
improvisations, postulate crashing
of spaces through spaces, by the armful,
by the second, metallurgic variations,
splashed black, inkless, mould and gleam,
the mercury skyline there
and nothing especially loaded,
even the drabness observed
to be less than especially drab.

*

What compunction in the incline,
mucose edging to a crystalline insignificance,
snails on the underside of the slab, to strive,
to verge on the plane of the actual would not signify,
however sincere, however established the incline,
slabbed snails stirring on the underside, makes you wonder,
do they winter, lay the slab gently, fit the slab
squarely back to its cavity in the earth,
the earth that grew to it.

*

What it was
was that we lived
and then it
wasn't

lived then it wasn't

we wasn't it lived

*

Unusual
sight to see,
the stairs in spate,
or does the novelty offend you,
cascade of flash-foam,
does the presentiment offend,
the froth that goes slinking with a smirk of sorts
from step to unthinkable step
in even this structure, home, this home, afloat
on the sewers, the labyrinth swollen,
floorboards a raft, the treading of water
a matter of more than mere routine,
our every solution to our effluent
outgrown us.

Welcome to the union of unions

First let me say what a privilege
most of us feel to have you with us at last,
especially when we hear you resisted so long.
And indeed to the point of affectation,
some might say. But ours is a broad church,
as you'll see. May I say you look well
and in full bloom. Had it been otherwise,
you might not have been invited. Joke,
of course. You've brought a towel, how kind.
We'll need it.
                Introductions, where to start.
Don't mind the oily rags, the overalls filing out
there – just been servicing the birthing pool
upstairs. You might need polythene shoe-covers
later. Try to step over, for now, or edge round it –
dummy or teat – and don't avert, she'll take it amiss;
the crawl-exhibit posture, pleats and seams extruded,
nothing shameful. Soil and swab of their communion,
spit-provider, as you were. On hands and knees behind the sofa
makes a threesome; breathe from the gut. Not gut,
I mean tummy. Speaking of which, the upgrade, bolted
to the wall, surround sound, footage beginning at eight
for the moral improvement of all spinsters,
showing a pulsing in membranous space. And see,
as a token of respect we've given the job
of holding the handset to her of the eightfold
contribution, she who clanks like a bag of old hammers
when she extricates what's left of herself
from the sling on the hoist to go milking
out in the shed. They like it alfresco
but the nights are drawing in now – cold,
don't you find? Your nipples at any rate seem
to think so. You might cover yourself –

exposure without legacy makes a whore,
some folks would say – but after all, here's where
such faults may be corrected. *Her* chap's a major player
in hedge funds, be in the cloakroom if not holding forth,
and he's tremendous fun in company,
doing his bit at the heart of the company, streaked
seed splashed across the tiles again, poor man,
been known to spend himself in his blood
in the name of the jar, for the sake of the legacy,
doing his bit. There'll be, if I know these good people
as well as I like to think I know these good people,
a decent whip-round before the night's done. And him
refusing every visual stimulus thus far known to man,
for love of his – her. Congrats all round. Perhaps
a modest donation, too, in support of the mass ovulation
project, sign the card. The work they do, we really feel it.
No, I mean really. First in months for that one
next to that one writhing on the slab in holy ecstasy –
a visionary pain, quite normal, you can't stop yourself
from looking. But my hands, I'm sure you've noticed,
have remained within my trousers all along. My speculum
ditto. Tell me: how long have you craved the rip
and the stitch? A small amount of fear is good, since fear
is natural and natural is good, and nothing unnatural
can have any place here. Glutting and rending and swelling
and suck the only weapons we have against total
abnegation. Take it from me. Long years
in the desert. You take it from me.

After that sojourn

What a great find – a model establishment –
potential for a bleary manual drilling of inspection holes
in the wallboards – this is a nocturne – steady the penlight –
turn the brace and press on hard, apply the crowbar
where your fingers feel the gap – remove with caution,
don't inhale, don't pause to wipe that from your eyes –
the unsound fixtures cracked and perishing – steady
the penlight – kill that penlight – only fibre optics
circulating life, the leaking valves are plainly audible –
tear out the insulation – gloves, what gloves – don't scratch,
ignore the welts you've raised, spit what you've crunched
and know that innovation costs, someone must pay for this,
or something must – procure the sleek and innocent,
let the sentence be commuted, shine that light again,
bear down and look, what slaughter, bats and moles
and birds and field mice, tagged unclassified,
fuse wire looped and twisted, metatarsals
jammed against the cutting, witness, hanged in rows
on clothes rails, and there's silence in the room –
or something like silence – but nothing
like quiet – go downstairs and tell the flunkey,
claim some vouchers, leave bad feedback,
do your worst.

Verbatim

The fissure in the stone, the stone itself,
provides no clue to what you're missing,
destination, sanctum, hole. Rain persists
in staying as far off as the road you will not
walk to, feints through its flannel-drab ruse
of a veil, and a wrought-iron gate is judged
to be brown with rust, uncontroversially
brown. Had there been little here to fall into,
now there is not. Stone is stone. This rain
is too small to absorb, to be absorbed by.
Yesterday's forecast was misguided. Clumps
of leaf-mulch, dried-out bleached stuff
at the roadside, are projection merely.
Unseen, flaking sparse, chimerical dust.

Expectorant

Let's not exaggerate
not about sickening ever so slightly
not exaggerate not about sickening
sickening ever so slightly with shame
the moment the gape becomes a gape
the gape dilating in its straining towards knowing
straining deeper into unknowing
too late to rescind the unspoken compact
when the commitment to speak is the compact
lodged in the gullet the gagging the blanching
was it shock the blanching shock or disappointment
let's not exaggerate not about shock let's not
exaggerate the virtues real or presumed
of spontaneity which is a certain kind of smoothness
in unknowing let's not sicken for the front wheel
hauled erect nor for the easy
confirmation of the error for the slither of opinions
dead fish spilled from the net on the quayside mouths wide open
for the fool with the slick moving lips
and the eyes of dead fish
whose words are the squits
who wants to see you swallow the bolus
in the hope of dislodging the bolus
no sense of sickening
no sense of shame in the eyes
of dead fish

Awash

Self-evidently thrilling
the resurgent gleaming world
no different from yesterday
except in slight accruals
of vast opportunity

drags its tidal waste the wrong way
up the gradient
all there is
prodigiously bulked with that which arguably isn't

could it be lethal
or is it simply what you hear
about how millions have been flat-packed
stacked in the freight shed
left to stew in their emissions
random pages of their strange redundant portfolios
rising to drift for a while on the surface
could it be lethal

all that mottle and sag (their hopes)
that proffer and squeeze (their endless hunger)
their implausible desires resolved as smarting expectation
could it be indemonstrably trivial

in this trembling street this morning
should there be cleansing in the updraught
in the waft of overripe camembert
in the stench of rotting whelks
should there be observance

Proposal for a superstructure

To live like ruminants – but no –
aren't they a bit rapey – stags, bulls, rams, etc. – rapey –
yes, a definite hint of rapiness in the herd –
you, call the vet out – clean the prod –

to live like ruminants – but gelded –
spayed and gelded – neutered ruminants –
with nothing but the cud –
prescription meds – you, where's that vet –

the cud – a landscape –
not disconsolate in bleakness – staring –
staring – without malice – artless indifference –
season giving way to season –

without market day –
the population dwindling – natural wastage –
field of your own – a copse – a brook –
the gentle rasp of old barbed wire –

a roll in the hay – a sniff at the ditch –
quick brush with the fence – slow trot to the byre –
dumb glance at the body in the long white coat
you trampled to death while grazing.

At the parting of the dogs

Mainly trying not to look.
Perhaps a tacit admission
that some kind of tacit admission
of guilt or complicity
would be welcome. Good
in the sense of assuaging
whatever it is
that hasn't quite managed
enough of itself
to justify being assuaged.
Scant relief
in the urge to share
for sharing's sake.

These people are human,
only human and not monsters,
the grins of the dogs
are superimposing what the people need to feel,
the dogs have failed to divine the purpose,
if there is a deeper purpose,
in the reassuring noises
of their owners, keepers,

being only dogs, without telepathy,
denied the relevant facts
and the ability
to shriek
with human voices,

though they do,
like kidnap victims. Panic,
swivelling eyes,
gram-negatives in the slobber,
frantic lapping at muzzle and nose
and the tongue of the other
and then round the gums,

and when the licking doesn't help
they lock in fast
with snout and maw,
nailed at the bite,
the people shrieking like the dogs.

No mobile phones were harmed
in the making of this picture. They have left
the auditorium and have taken their owners with them
and the fates of all involved
remain unknown.

Dialogic

But it's your duty
you whose duty is to strip
to bare the preselected razored disinfected
plucked and bleached in preparation
for the stylus or the inkjet or the laser
you whose duty is to yield
so we can speak our right to speak
so we can scrawl our shrieking edicts
on your strangely shrinking skin and keep on scrawling
some from memory some from someone else's memory
others plagiarizing some old slob's most intimate
tattoos deformed predictably by suppurating
crops of cellulitis no-one urging us to leave your epidermis
to the comfort of superfluity to shrinkage in the weeds
at the edge of the pool where your faithful bundle
goes on mouldering no-one urging us to master the craft
of manufacturing vellum for our scrawling too consumptive
too indicative of what was once at stake and might be still
and too much time to peg it all out and some of the pigments
highly toxic shame that all you really wanted was to exercise
the right you thought a right the right
to efface yourself or failing that erase yourself
on terms you once made up
and you think this small
request unfair?

Posterity, here, for all good people, now

And not just roped in
for the long, demanding haul,

to take whatever comes, to loom
below the fistular pathology

of the almost-certain future.
Celebrate, yes, but please

liaise with my fiancé first,
my puking spouse-to-be,

on how the forms don't fit, on how
we've gone syncretic

but the forms still don't quite
fit. How do the earnest

like to put it, this tradition,
in their best speaking voices on phones,

is it *affianced*? What a pledge:
to coexist in such conditions,

which presume a gentle
biodegradation

and a general lack
of haemorrhaging,

old chattels going for scrap
without complaint.

Back when you ceased to laud the tendency
of things that pass

to pass into the next-best place to nothing
(smaller chance of endless concretizing,

smaller chance of shame),
you could have cacked your pants for joy,

but they were looking,
they could see.

*

All I know is
that it starts to give offence,

when does it start
to give offence,

how don't they like it
up your way,

now that you've trodden good and hard
in what you've spilled,

now that you've varnished your opinions
and the faces of your children,

now that everyone's a business doing business
in the spilled guts of the business,

now that someone else has shown your unkempt
anus in the window,

will your shop be boarded up,
your assets seized,

or will you liquidize
before they get the word,

you've packed a suitcase
and you're waiting for the call

but no-one's calling,
ingrates all,

and after everything you did
to keep them safe, on side,

certificates of excellence
in growing people

browning
on the wall.

*

We cocked a snook at them, the neighbours
on their planet. Cocked a snook,

they didn't notice but we saw it
and we put it on the planet, there were dangers,

controversial things and dangers, oral flora,
but we toothed it, toothed that snook

before we cocked it. They've a marriage,
fact and pseudo-, all our neighbours on their planet,

and we toothed it, and they filed it
and they didn't even notice that we'd seen it

as they filed it, oral flora. Fact and pseudo-,
they've a marriage, controversial things

and dangers and we've cocked it,
they've a planet and we filed it,

cocked our flora on their controversial
oral, fact and pseudo-, didn't notice,

toothed their marriage planet, snooked it,
dangers, controversial, seen.

Didactic

To footle about in the world, declining its verb
of choice, whatever came top, *to engage*,
entails a certain enantiodromia, quaint at a push –
remark, a faint sensation of badness –
insofar as anything's possible, really, at all.

Or, put simply, things have somehow simply
gone on being got done, and those who let them
be got done are doing their duty, though their use
of passive constructions can be reductive and they can't
control their children, birth rates, dogs.

And there's simply no alternative. We tried
to find a grammar free of indicatives,
structuring only in the conditional, positing nothing
that couldn't be reified, canonized, praised
in the past subjunctive, but we heard

that there'd been ructions – enemy
acrobats tumbling in, a number of dirty words
and ways of doing rude things dying in custody,
not to mention the first-person singular going to war
with the first-person plural, even the cleverest
private transport solutions falling out of the sky,

they say it was terrible. Please
remind us who they were. What sick
compendium they crawled from.
Why we bothered to take them seriously.
Contributors may rest assured
that each and every submission
will be closely read and carefully
assessed by our panel of experts

but should kindly note
the prize draw has now closed.

Z new observance

And at length it
had nothing to say.
Or found it had
lost what there was
to be said. What
had there been,
ever. Only raindrops
scoring tracks
amid the frigid and the clinging,
that jittery zigzag they beetled,
strange contrast. That,
and monumental arrogance,
brash caprice. Such easy disgust
for the bourgeois termagant,
puffed-up pastry,
raking the drawers to cull
his mite-infested underpants,
how unlikely now
the shuffled pack of assorted
fun prophylactics,
more relief
in the simple immediacy
of drops
emitted in sequence,
sotto voce,
from his pap-like tawny
genital
into the mythos,
how could the toilet be
his life's most diligent
chronicler,

whomsoever, what,
the which of it
never established,
now as back then
emphatically not –
not – up for discussion.

Where is it, that silence

Silence haltingly
assembled under the eyeball
or behind it, somewhat grudgingly
projected onto the membrane, piece by piece,
hypothesis only, rather jealously
cupped in the palm and held to the pupil,
still in fragments, held too late
in bits to the earhole –

silence that elongates
the last complaint of the tuning fork
they thumped into the lawn as though for a croquet game,
the crew that had no mallet to break a finger with,
or a back – or was it for use in fact as a tent peg,
though they hadn't so much as a flysheet
a threesome could frolic under, grunting
like murderous fuck –

silence that elongates
the brunt of the blast, the spewing
of stones in the slew of the speeding diesel,
clank of the trailer yanked through the dark
to the mythical crossroads (sooner or later
someone won't be coming home,
will not be spotted from the driveway,
someone somewhere will be sad) –

silence that elongates
to tinnitus in its own absence, as though
it were nowhere, even as though it were plausibly
never – it might have been never – although
it was noted in passing,
encouraged a little,
seemed
kind.

Gesture

If a grin could be produced here
it would seem cossetted in the making
and condemnable – no-one to see
but the bearer plainly liable, aware
of that liability. Still there is ease
in what acceptance of boredom
brings, a light astonishment
tending to blank in the act, remarkable
fact of not knowing. Today is unlikely
to be the last day and if there are people
in the distance then it is unlikely that
they are imagined. It would seem
cossetted otherwise. Heads and hands
just visible. Someone is laughing.

www.ingramcontent.com/pod-product-compliance
Lightning Source LLC
Chambersburg PA
CBHW052137010526
44113CB00036B/2291